GATHER ING VIEW

POEMS

JACK C. BUCK

Punch Drunk Press Ltd.

Denver, Colorado

For information, address:

Punch Drunk Press Ltd.

PO Box 9435

Denver CO 80209

Interior Design: Brice Maiurro

Cover Design: Samantha Hester

Library of Congress Control Number:

2018943549

Buck, Jack

Gathering View / Jack C. Buck 1st Ed.

ISBN - 978-0-9988902-3-4

Also by Jack Buck

Deer Michigan (Truth Serum Press)

will you let it send you out (Ghost City Press)

Acknowledgements

I would like to thank the editors of the following journals, where some of the poems in this book first appeared, sometimes in different forms:

Boston Accent Lit, Great Lakes Review, The Tishman Review, Ginger Collect, Five 2 One, Tuck Magazine, (b)OINK Zine, Fourth and Sycamore

PUNCH DRUNK PRESS

PUNCH DRUNK PRESS LTD

DENVER CO

TABLE OF CONTENTS

THE FIELD

a welcome disorientation of where we physically are | 3

emerge into light let this light fill us |4

depending what question you ask of it | 5

gathering view | 6

the sum total of how we live our lives | 7

and it sounds like this | 8

towards | 9

a needed belief | 10

everything is something else before it's not | 11

if you could find this place you could believe again | 12

what comes after | 13

its effect is temporary | 14

send forward | 15

the part we can't see | 16

persistent illusion systematically developed | 17

in defense of acting with little thought to it | 18

when everything was always good | 19

Michigan 1993 | 20

physical sound of our reflection | 21

a long loving look | 22

it doesn't mean a lot but it does | 23

the marriage of football and September | 24

hail mary poem | 25

autumn before winter | 27

making it to the end | 28

WHERE WE WERE HERE BEFORE

into | 33

was | 34

light | 35

our | 36

is | 37

a past version of its love | 38

to remember | 39

to give us | 40

above / beneath | 41

where | 42

remembering while we are living in it | 43

all | 44

just as there's value in staying | 45

another winter poem | **46**

summer of love | **48**

sometimes it means nothing and... | **49**

from before | **50**

a silent way | **51**

meet there yourself | **53**

to go | **54**

WE SAVE US

we are water | **59**

become something new | **60**

into the great wide open | **61**

we save us | **62**

from the last time | **63**

what ends is a beginning | **64**

you're missing | **65**

environmental politics | **66**

the promised land | **67**

volunteers | **69**

low murmur of conversation over water | **70**

before I ever went and saw the desert | **71**

to begin again | **72**

our measure | 73

being trees | 75

call it by its name | 77

making distance | 78

glory days | 79

having breakfast in a parking lot at sunrise | 80

in the ending | 81

rise | 82

for my family and friends

Gathering View

Jack C. Buck

The Field

a welcome disorientation of where we physically are

from afar the fans

rise in unison as if

rooting together

emerge into light let this light fill us

and with a good wind we are lifted beyond

or whatever you call the rush of air on you

soaring through the air

even if for a moment

sitting in our seats

a temporary lapse of gravity

depending of what question you ask of it

measured by inches

the placement of decision

so close either way

gathering view

to feel the outside

we have protested the roof

our hands touch the sky

the sum total of how we live our lives

setting the record straight

one way or another

all will be asked to explain

what they've done and why

and it sounds like this

marching bands in sound

us humming in tune

feeling a part of something

we have found what we were looking for

towards

to haul your body

push the spirit of youth through the air towards a goal

begin with a foot

then a yard

you can't go any further unless you go through it

with time all the way

a needed belief

no way to move forward without formation of others

with self like that of a river

rivers to converge

forming the largest river of all

which was not there but there now

with each day we deliberately venture a little further

believing there to be a point one reaches to cross

propelled by hands and feet

hold on to one another

in this shared life

everything is something else before it's not

the roar of you onward

dragging the weary body back and forth

in soul through mud our shadows

stealing the color of the field

this time of the year

there is only hard dirt and coming winter

as a body is gracefully hurled through the air

if you could find this place you could believe again

perhaps it means more

in the towns to be able to compete

against gigantic cities

across the way

with what seems like an unlimited number of players

on behalf of those places some of us have lived

or you have passed through

a pushback of the city's great noise caused by restlessness

and commerce

the best places are nowhere we have ever been

what comes after

down field from a distance

it looks as if a whale

has been strategically placed

across the midpoint of the field

obstructing the view to shore

standing in water rising

somebody has suggested we gently climb atop

to have a look around

side by side

above the great white whale

to see what we should do next

its effect is temporary

in a slow wave breaking the shore

crashing the wall of strong human force

a heaving swell inflating the air around us

they attempt to sink an inflated ball below the surface

send forward

by any means necessary

as long as it does not lead to death

something fell to the ground

and was picked up and kept on going

like that of a savior

they carry whatever is left of themselves

through the streets to the markers at each end of town

the part we can't see

facing one another in parallel lines

coming together someone has decided to toss a ball

I'm exhausted by cruelty

a momentary agreement of peace

another has agreed to play catch and to throw back

it feels important and necessary to keep this going

however long even forever if it is needed

until we are told to stop

persisted illusion systematically developed

back then in school

afflicted with all that stored up competition

began roaming around wondering what to do with it all

a bold figure away from home

with their newly found freedom

maybe it's America's rite of passage

in this human way

in defense of acting with little thought to it

down and distance

reached incrementally

in the big field of beautiful expansive earth

with much interference along

in need of persistence to move ahead

the curious thousand ways everywhere

our innate desire for change

too much emphasis on decision leads one from

what we need of carefree adolescence

find your way through moving water

will you let it send you out a changed thing

when everything was always good

I am young

at the time my father is not yet old

my mother is always young

a late November afternoon between rain and snow

gray sky

dark enough to have the lights on

I'm cold without knowing it

Michigan 1993

in the far corner the crowd of students

in unison rise in architectural grandeur

bent forward in ready stance

arms stretched towards the field in ritual

my eyes follow watching the movement of the teams

I believe everywhere in the world people are wearing

layers underneath jackets

the other team

that drove up from Iowa doesn't stand a chance

just look at us

we have mothers & fathers

taking their sons

and daughters to their first game on our side

physical sound of our reflection

from neighboring driveways and front lawns

announcing the start of the game the band begins

we sing, I echo we, you echo me

welcoming the change from

spending most of our lives in quiet

a long loving look

another reason to get together

I lean in close in autumn light

it doesn't mean a lot but it does

summer is summer

and summer some more

one can almost not remember

when the day is its own way

in reaction the light dims

and the heat

eventually turns into a box of basement sweatshirts

with relief and welcome the beginnings of autumn

where you know fall

we open the window to let in all the air

the whole town and church

including the good people skipping out on church

and everyone shopping in the market

takes on hope of what might be

the marriage of football and September

for a good prayer

for a better look we go outside

how much of tradition is relation of time and season

hail mary poem

there is a secret in everything

half the game is spent living in a poem

on a cloud that's lightly raining

during a magnificent symphony

just making people aware of the beauty of it

sometimes when I am staring at a wall or a door or

when I am around hundreds of strangers in a public place

waiting at a 5 o'clock red light

I wonder what the world could be like

if everyone wrote and read poetry to each other

like what if all the people

flung their doors open and got out of their cars

and the force of good words

and actions literally pulled us forward

all of us from the soles of our shoes

what if poems and art provided what

was missing from our lives

how do we ask the questions that force the reflection

we are to each other what we will get

it seems so obvious thinking about it

believing this can't only be it

knowing there's still so much we can do

for one another

autumn before winter

football is nearly over

the trees are void of this season thinking now of what's left

and the walk through university campus

has become a slow conversation

you can tell by the lapse

in Saturday afternoons being put away under a sink

I once said to you

that autumn is the best thing to say to you

across a field in the woods

the air is cold with the coming idea of long sweeps of snow

reaching us in distance from the lake

making it to the end

end of the season one last hurrah

we run through our neighborhood

knocking on doors

to collect all the city's candy in a pillowcase

wearing an oversized worn out football uniform

with a helmet that hurts from no inner padding

in between houses with turned off lights

I take off the helmet for a brief moment

for relief I blow on my nearly frozen fingers

to cup my raw numb ears

it's getting late and the cold rain is coming down

I run as fast as we can

as the echo of a make believe crowd cheers

seeking distances we've never been able to reach

all the way

Where We Were Here Before

into

shadows come into themselves
where at night the light meets our winter bodies

around a small wood table
we are leaning in close gathering
giving our space to the distance outside

the town closes in collecting all that space
outside the white fields expand out

all snow and wind
eight years of distance
it's impossible to see anything else as we
draw into one another

was

those summer evenings to live for
where fate made a point are gone
as the years
slip into another oncoming year

all that time
spent together when we were young has passed too

we are much older now
where our once love is replaced by others
who think they know what to do with it

we are defined by nothing
but the ever faint memory
till someday it is never known by anyone left

running its course of time
love was
where we were here before

light

image
of light in the morning
even in the winter woods
slowly reaching each dark angle of shadow
before anyone has opened their eyes
our word for
morning
sudden

our

our not love is
thinking of one another
at the quiet
in between moments of our days
while at the same time
thinking if we say anymore of it
it will become love
a love that could one day stop
so if we never allow it to begin with
it has no way of ever ending

is

how short can a love story be
and still be considered a love story
the distinction of time
putting value in terms of weighed quality
time's insistence to prove it exists
believing in itself so wholly
there are limits to all of this
to say what love is

a past version of its love

compared to feeling in time before
thoughts they seem to have come from
form that did not ever fit us
not like then
you now seem too distant
even lost now
I still contain a place where it still loves
if ever so small we have now become

to remember

as if all of life is like this
as if knowing life is not like this
to know now when a day is really a good one
and so you try your best to remember
where afterwards you can return again

to give us

such time preserves
if not us
and all of this
love survives itself
where we had tried

above/beneath

today is a tundra
where all the good and happiness of
yesterday is -256 frozen
tomorrow is running water

where

where the heat of our bodies meets the cold architecture of
the lake
back there
where we come from
together years later in another city in mountain land
from this distance we tried
to make it what we thought it had ought to be

remembering while we are living in it

the first loss is like shadows everywhere
depending on who's doing the remembering
the first love is not like that at all

sometimes it means nothing now
and sometimes it feels like everything

there's a chance for us
if we once and for all decide to forget
what everyone else has already told us
of what it's supposed to be like
only then
we might live there forever

I'm hoping that
everything I don't know
is as real as everything I do know

all

what was the value
everything and again
all the time what time
that amount when people say forever
what is it about the end of one time
and the beginning of another
once more
I gather all that is needed
of what might be

just as there's value in staying

it is best at night with the snow coming down
to walk through the wide empty streets
or to stay right where we are
just on the other side of all that cold
like migration being an effect of winter not all birds leave

when you can't remember when it wasn't
with the life you wanted

from here a sense of scale
its effect from the greater distance
and with everything quiet that can't happen in summer

with the proximity of others
which I'm not sure is possible in many circumstances
a reason to come nearer
sitting across a small table our hands can touch

it's worth being cold for that
is it snowing where you are
losing track of days

another winter poem

north wind blows all the kids to the ground
they're seen clinging to the hard dirt
crawling back home to safe shelter
for everyone who's been here awhile
knows what's coming

I inherit the love of woods among winter
where the snow arrives early and stays late
you can tell by the red of our faces
fully committed we take in the cold

I'm going out for a while to help myself
therefore everyone around me
I shovel all the snow of outside
up & down & across
I've given away all remaining desire to be somewhere else
see the outline of yourself in a space of forever
here along the lake from where I've left

a lake is not a car
a lake is not a job nor a way to pay the bills
it's not like we can disguise lake water
and go up to a merchant and use it as a legitimate currency
it's more than that

winter is such perfection
up here it's difficult to describe
heard complaints are to be attributed to a
misunderstanding of seasons
in heaven there'll be a time of winter

with everything else in life going fast
this slows it down
providing an unmentioned rhythmic quality
like a kid lightly hammering a nail
into one of the trees out back

in the repetition of snow
finally we are stopped

summer of love

it snows in my poems of my life
as it snows on the open fields of Northern North America

and at the end of your street
where we can no longer see out the window

below we sleep naked on top of the bed covers
in the summer of our love in January
where our love could swim
across all 148 miles of Lake Michigan in the cold
defying all commonplace weather of logic and reason
and science and math
a steady thriving and building
where the mirror of the shore wears out eventually
disappearing entirely

we swim out forever
with the rear view of our lives
getting smaller and larger at once

sometimes it means nothing and sometimes it feels like everything

the first loss is like shadows everywhere
depending on who's doing the remembering
the first love is not like that at all

from before

I am on the other side of the country years passed
things not remembered or
never thought of after come back
as the cities grow larger in size
of buildings and people
towns grow deliberately smaller
you come back to this place
in low silence
giving us to notice its own form
you can tell in places like this
as we commit with what we know
slowly it stays with you more with distance

a silent way

the ground is tough
to bury any bodies this time of the year
the coordination of successful planning is formidable
early June is when people can be seen out there
with their loved ones digging their grave

it's best after a week of early summer rain
nine outta ten times it's still snowing some in April
otherwise everyone would start earlier to get it over with
if one could help it they would hold out as long as possible
and wait till July so as not to inconvenience anyone
we all try
sometimes you can't go on any longer though
even as much as you want
it's one's time

there's real meaning in acceptance
you're half in this world and half in the other
nothing to do now but let the soul take over

sadly we have it backwards
most of the time in this situation the person dying
is just looked at as old and that's that
what a scary silent way
on an evolutionary timeline
you'd think we would've figured out more by now
one cold morning

way out in only natural sound
you know why you are there
it's mid-March and the ground is frozen
and it was snowing as it is

meet there yourself

it has been snowing for five months
inside another long impressive winter
that we will no doubt endure
a steady unrelenting build up
11 degrees that feels like 11 degrees
everyday this time of the year
yet we are remarkably healthy in spirit
given the circumstances
saying things you never knew you knew
an optimum environment
for what we're going for out here
not much to do but walk down to the bar
and talk life of the mind
for the next five months on dollar beer night
which is everynight in places like this
hadn't thought about ever leaving before
meet there yourself

to go

just before winter
five birds land up high on their usual spot
I can see them
clearly this time of the year of the bare branches
they are chatting to one another about the usual stuff

after some time the birds and I are motionless
as a silent cold gust of wind comes upon us
bending the branches of the tree just enough
I shiver at the sight of it
I notice people have begun to head towards home

sitting at the usual park bench
I roll my neck back to look straight up to the sky
and suddenly
with all the indications of the last five minutes
the first bird lifts and starts
and another and another has a go
as if for a moment they thought about it
as if they were ever meant to stay

We Save Us

we are water

where the lake people
of Minnesota Wisconsin Michigan
sway together along the shoreline
wait to enter after this life
I am only now beginning to know
drawn to water
standing before the rhythmic roll of the waves
coming up on our knees
we look across the shore over the sound
in that way everyone does
when they are in the presence of a large body of water
as if it was possible to see all the way
to the bottom if we committed enough
under all this water there's a door to go through

become something new

if you keep walking eventually you can become snow
it takes a while though
if you don't walk long enough you end up getting too cold
and wanting to turn back
worse yet if you're really far out
past that dividing line
you run the risk of dying on the walk back
instead it's better to just keep on going
best of all when you turn into winter
you eventually turn into spring
and who knows what the possibilities are
when that happens
only spring and you will know
the answer to that great one
and maybe better than best of all
you will know the answer to a question
that none us who stayed back will ever know

into the great wide open

the cathedral factories rise like western peaks
instead of traditional steel and bad air
good thing we can see Lake Michigan
otherwise we wouldn't stand a chance
Chicago the great northern winter in cold slow moving
there's not much to mourn for adios then
although what about those broken windows
for all that they've done
at near dawn when they climbed up the walls and
out the windows in a dream daze
the ones who found a way
the others only to awaken once again
to find beyond the day another day
who never not hear the hum of machines in their heads
trusting nothing more than the hours
it was hard to believe
there were other places one could go to
elsewhere other than here

we save us

its sleek head is turned on its side in an unnatural way
looking like it has been snapped by some sort of machine
not of an animal's doing
there is a result to all of this
its eyes close more than they are open
I crouch down now palms on the ground
watching to imitate its labored breathing
believing if I can just keep on breathing
this will take a long time
the rain has been coming down steady for hours
we are trying to save us

from the last time

occurring in a kitchen
framed by a window
above a sink
it's pouring in this town
that used to be all woods
taking over the remainder of evening
a beautiful woman
we are married two children
in front of me
her back towards me
I just about reach her
to place my hand on her shoulder
I want her to be her
the house fades
is elsewhere with decision
with no one out on the road
the traffic light blinking
is still probably blinking
standing in the middle of the street
the one thing you can at least go back to
you can see clearly her face from before

what ends is a beginning

the day the snow finally melts
and you can see the grass again
like a forgotten memory
even though the high of the day is only 45
and it's already late April
it feels very much like mid-June
with the breeze sweeping across the lake
accompanied with the sun
the whole town comes out to gather in their front yards
disoriented from spending too much time in winter
some of us can be seen out in the middle of the road
cheering like wild animals that want to be turned loose
time stands still
we dance, round and round, in the warm spring air
just in time
another three weeks of not having this
the whole place would've gone clinically insane
everybody takes off work
we turn off the tv
the mail is put on hold
there's no war
friend and foe shake hands in fair compromise
no one in charge is trying to pull one over on anybody
all the old promise of spring has come back for a day
calling attention to itself
from the sight of fields of green

you're missing

go my friend
become the shape of a freewheeling unknown river
disguised as a creek
then reappear
so we catch a glimpse of you in ceaseless flow
release yourself from the cycle of incarnation
become another for which you want to be
incrementally always be becoming
do not return this way
save yourself in turn to save the rest of us
after you die the emails and junk mail will keep on coming
go with buddha
go with poem
you're halfway there
lead the way
more of us will follow in time
relinquish the trappings of our world
yes
you're really doing it
wait
not yet
come back
we need you

environmental politics

in a past life
my friends and I
made really cool bad poor quality videos
of our favorite songs played over footage of nature
usually it was some sort of ambient track
for example there would be a shot of a slow going stream
then a quick jerk of the camera to zoom in
on the canopy of the forest swaying in the wind

the internet is wild now
but it was real wild back then
it was the new frontier
it was a free for all
the internet made you think you could do anything
we were insane enough back then
to think we could save the world
if we could just make enough of those music/nature videos
then maybe we could influence the collective
and the sub atomic wavelength particles of you and me
would all of a sudden become one universe in itself
we would awaken the world to our new belief
we were convinced we were going to save it all

the promised land

last night I sang karaoke with Bruce Springsteen
and all my friends

even the friends I haven't seen in 15 years
living across the country were there
it was like we never left
but still gained all of that good stuff you get
by going away

I knew every single word to all of the songs despite always
being terrible at remembering specific words of when and
where they are supposed to go in line

it was all happening
in the living room of my grandparent's house
during the night's intermission

I must have spent a good 30 minutes
trying to describe to everyone
the time my grandmother and I went driving
all around the state
to buy this specific living room rug

Bruce was by the sink in the kitchen
making cocktails for everyone
at the same sink where the ghost of my grandmother
makes cocktails on Christmas

for reasons not explained
we didn't want our feet to touch the floor
my friends were attempting to save me from the ground
by hoisting me in a chair
to lift me through the ceiling
they couldn't come with me though

they never said why and I never asked
I just knew deep down they weren't
so I didn't want to bring it up
and make all of us feel sad and awkward about it all

everyone in the room was telling me that I could go now
if I wanted
that it would be safe
and I would feel better in a way I've never known
they said this other place was better than all of the
best karaoke bars
in the history of all karaoke bars

that sure sounded like a place to check out
but I didn't want to go yet
I wanted to stay with my friends
and sing some more songs
and here we still are

volunteers

the National Parks are being sold off
to the highest bidder and being paved
into giant parking lots
we are in need of volunteers
to come eat sand and swallow the river
in order to store what we can
until we figure out what to do
and/or where we are going to put what's left of it
we are asking to tell all your friends

low murmur of conversation over water

an aggressively uncommercial cup of water
is the star of an ongoing play
taking place in a small beautiful theater
more specifically in a remote fishing cabin
more accurately in the figurative space of the audience's
memory

it's sort of a gothic tale
about the influence of our human decisions
the action which occurs
over the course of the 40 minute duration of the play
describes the ritual of water

the main character of the play
doesn't come across necessarily cynical
(collective consciousness of those
in attendance/theatergoers keep the water level
from evaporating)

outside in the lobby
attendees stand in a windowless room
exchanging comment over tables
placed with empty water glasses
to remind them of what used to be there

before I ever went and saw the desert

     I was in a library researching alternative ways
to the business of self understanding
studying up on the ways of eastern philosophy

     reading the moving clouds
across the plains

   later on
       only to find that most of them writing the books
       died from some avoidable bad habit
       they never bothered mentioning

"Yeah, he was kind of a jerk. To be honest,"
     a friend would say

that was sorta a good time to be living in America

     for the most part
despite all that's been going on for all this time
even today

     really what do you expect
       what year is it
          are we now the ones knowing

     we know a little bit more now than then
not much

to begin again

on a high ledge
with all that space below
decision should be kept to a minimum
otherwise everyone/everything will stay remained
and not every poem is about potential leaps to death
from people waiting in line
claiming to be of the enlightened
believe it or not
some of us want to go on singing
knowing it's important
even when ourselves and others don't want to

our measure

inside large windows of morning light
we learn measurements
how a ruler works
and what the different units mean in the world

the kids walk around the classroom
pacing out in large step

what's the perimeter of your desk in inches
measure your favorite classroom plant in centimeters
(Can't decide which one you like best of all?
That's a good thing. Measure them all then)

using a meter stick, let's see how tall you are
compare yourself to a plant
how many plants stacked up are you

with your new found data
based on your own height
provide a reasonable estimate
of how tall our whole class is as a giant
would we reach the top of the school's roof
the sun

off to the side
a small group of students have begun making a human
ladder

they are now standing on each other's shoulders
together they are reaching beyond measure

being trees

what if we grow tired
the point wasn't to come out here for a test
but staring at a group of black oak trees up in Minnesota
for a four and half days in just about silence
will give us a good idea if we have what it takes to make it

we aren't standing around to impose our will/philosophies
on Minnesota
or anyone or any place
we are here to watch
what it takes to live time like the trees do
that means good growth
without adding any further interpretation to it:
this is a forest
that is a tree
this is my hand touching a tree

this isn't easy despite what one may think
it's not simply sitting in a chair
staring for hours at a cathedral of trees
while taking notes
and sketches to take back with us
to spread the good word

time passes in this type of time in this space
eventually we say to each other
okay we can be trees

we both agree
after that
we drive around the rest of America
to decide where we want to be trees together

call it by its name

in the evenings we walk in the park

how a person walks can tell a lot about that person
I tend to walk a little quicker than you

when I am with you
I match your pace and slow down
allowing ourselves to take more notice along the way

from back there to here
I take in double the amount of life

leading beside always a foot just behind me
you place your hand on my shoulder for me to stop
for a minute as you tell me about the flowers
giving their proper names

this reminds us
of that one poem
you had taped on your fridge back in the day
where it lists off the names of everything it sees hears and
feels

we are reminded of which poem this reminds us of

making distance

too late now for
could've been best versions of ourselves
so whatever the solution to that is we need to figure out

suffering the perfect loss
there was nothing to say about it more
better to do something about it instead

since then
unrelenting pure joy I've almost entirely forgotten
a decade now later
putting necessary distance between me and
things/people/events

that necessity of continuing progression of distance
one time I drove across America
to the farthest point I could possibly go
what a life I forgot

glory days

boys run
in stride
as if practicing the sport of staying alive

what we believed
the faster you jump over the family plots
the better off one was of not getting dragged under

the old man who lived at the corner
we thought to be bad insane
us too young to know the difference
he dead in sleep midweek last winter
no one knowing until the snow being three foot high

we believe in curses and prayers
and superstition and good luck and bad luck
with one foot landed the other lifted off the ground
already going ahead not one of us stupid enough to stop
for a moment to catch our breath
they'll take you down below and replace you
take your soul and body

what everybody in the neighborhood says goes
there and then summer went on good
we anything but dead

having breakfast in a parking lot at sunrise

       still not having gone to sleep
with soft morning sound of light on the 17 barns I counted
one day on the road heading west out of town
the occasional car with someone inside commuting to their
job 30 miles south

       asking if I want to walk with you
down to the grocery store to pick up some breakfast for
everyone still asleep

       it's the 15th of the month payday

       it's just after six in the morning
when the day is deciding what it wants to do with this one
life

       later on 80 degrees late afternoon thunderstorm
but that's a long ways away
we will be wonderfully asleep by then
skipping over the normalcy of a Tuesday
knowing years from now we will feel like we are missing
something

       times like these when the obligations of a day
were going for a long walk
and seeing where it would lead

in the ending

     their faces and eyes and chests spectacular
above their heads
heaven
nearby just out of their sight

     they walk beside the other
positioning themselves in a constant
never a day/night unclaimed or left unturned

     fearless
in all the good ways

     not yet other separate lives
before them not together
elsewhere
good thing
otherwise together they would've been obliterated by one
and another

     outside in the middle of the street
the outlines of their figures
stretch 20 yards in front shaped in a curve
trapped forever
between angles and light
with other selves waiting to take their place

rise

three feet of my body already exists underground
I walk around like that
not many people notice besides other undergrounders
yesterday I saw a guy trudging along up to his ears in dirt
I said hello to him but he couldn't hear me

I want to rise to the surface of the leaves of October
I don't even have to get up all the way to the leaves still on
the trees
I will start at ground level and go from there
with time maybe I can reach the height of a flower
a tree
a really tall old tree
a let go balloon
the space between canopy and bird
high sky
until I am ready to be bird
I'll fly away
cloud
space
gone

About the Author

Jack C. Buck, originally from Michigan, now lives and teaches in Denver, Colorado.

www.ingramcontent.com/pod-product-compliance
Lightning Source LLC
Chambersburg PA
CBHW032145040426
42449CB00005B/411